Sleepwalking Again

Sleepwalking Again

Poems by

John Raffetto

Cover design by Shay Culligan
Cover image by Laura Cleffmann on Unsplash
Chapter 1–5 images from Unsplash,
respectively by godsfavoriteart,
2, Public Domain Vectors,
Jess Bailey, and Da Vector
Author photo by John Raffetto

ISBN: 979-8-90146-820-3

Kelsay Books
502 South 1040 East, A-119
American Fork, Utah 84003
Kelsaybooks.com

for Kathy and Michael

Acknowledgments

Special thanks to all the editors at the following publications, where most of the poems in this book first appeared:

Adelaide Literary Magazine
Ariel Chart International Journal
The Balloon
Better Than Starbucks Poetry and Literary Journal
BlazeVOX Journal
Bristol Noir
Clockwise Cat Literary Magazine
Coldnoon Journal
Down in the Dirt Magazine
Evening Street Press and Review
Fish Food Magazine
Literary Orphans
Lothlorien Poetry Journal
Magnolia Review
Midwest Quarterly Literary Magazine
Mojave River Review
Olentangy Review
Outlaw Poetry
Penwood Review
Poetry Quarterly
Red Fez Magazine
Westward Quarterly Magazine
Wilderness House Literary Review
Write City Magazine
Young Ravens Literary Review

Special loving thanks to Kathy Bergen for her support, suggestions, and editing expertise.

Contents

CHAPTER 3

CHAPTER 4

CHAPTER 5

CHAPTER 1

Sleepwalking

Sleepwalking
through murky walls
past beta waves into
a vivid ray—
an altered void of voids
suddenly slammed shut
door locked and bolted
hammered tight
between slate skies on desert plateaus.

Sleepwalking again
into twilight
avoiding night
that endless planet
where winds howl near
all sleepwalkers,
who decide to rest,
prop their heads
then observe a soft ballet of apparitions.

Utah Night Sky

Night sky meditation
as stars move in slow circles
of eternal movements
in dancing light.
The raven air crisp as a prophet.

A fallen moon with soft craters
is alive
at my feet
swallowed
by red stars
of constellations,
as vast galaxies
scatter light upon pines.

Solitary radiance
penetrate sandstone canyons
where time dissolves,
surrenders to a swamp of green fossils
under a half moon
casting a vacant luminosity.

Night Poems

It's late as I spin fragments and
cut-ups into streams of lapsed consciousness
laid out in blank verse
of staggered lines and prose.
A fountain of remorse excavated into
ashes of the dead.
A pause during insomnia
when the ebony sky oblivious to a last train
shaking creosote ties and bashful steel into the wee hours.

In the morning as sunlight reflects on amber walls
despair vanishes into stuttering words
abandoned for now in daylight.

Nocturnal Fever

The coyotes prowl in the city park
after people depart.
Their green eyes illuminate the night
searching for a stray
a loner left behind.
The people are asleep yet the coyotes roam.

The streetlights reflect jagged shadows
under an immense moon obscured by clouds,
as cottonwood trees convey
a lurking of nocturnal fever
breaks before daylight fading
into pale blue sky.

Nevada Neon

Dust upon a
Greyhound windshield
smeared green reflection
where mind clouds surge into town.
Mountain backbone of flight
as Carlos Castaneda strolls the neon strip
watching Las Vegas Show Girls
and peyote slot machines.

In a sightless evening he
reaches beyond cactus silhouettes
and shattered light,
running in darkness
trusting the oneness
while fools on the strip believe
there is nothing more.

Firefly Evening

Alone in dusky forest
as fireflies
cover my face
flashing like a yellow construction sign.

Splintered hickory bark
hangs from my arms,
poison ivy tendrils
climb around my bare legs,
a rash decision
to hop a boxcar
in the middle of the night
heading to Montana
alone with homeless men
eating dented cans of beans
huddled around the torn soul.

At the Oregon junction
I unfasten the coupling hitch
from the remainder of the train
and roll downhill toward
topaz mountains of craggy
Pacific shore,
coming to a
rolling stop
past a suite of clouds
as fireflies vanish.

Invasive Accident

Tree frogs staccato night echo.
Tree frogs without fear
surrender to Pacific rain or dry air—
starless clouds surround the evening and
chant a holy ritual in tropical breath,
an elementary lesson in native lands
where the stars are invisible
as tree frogs were once in Hawaii.

Now an invasive accident
deceive visitors
who marvel at the
staccato night echo.

All Night

Endless night of a dissolved sunset
as shadowless windows open without a breeze
or glow over the fierce night.
Ticking through the dusk,
coughing and difficult to breathe,
talking to the ceiling again
searching for a remedy of this reclining madhouse.

All I want is sleep,
but a thousand nails
have hammered my eyelids open.

The alley is blind without lights in webbed shadows
as petrified darkness near the edge of an abyss.
A time warp collapses in a fevered dream
twisted into a panicked elixir
and the sudden purge
of another incessant night.

I need sleep that keeps
wandering away for a drink
at a 4am bar
looking for action
near a quiet street
easing into
a carnival evening—
the only game in town.

Nobody's Tavern

The sputtered mirage ended abruptly as I
walk uphill in North Beach
trying to step out of my cold grip
into an all-night diner eating alone,
while she sleeps with her new husband.

Tangled in an edgy evening,
a journey down a darkened street—
the master's class of sharp desire.
Jukebox music blasts out of an open doorway—
jazz sonnets play as no one listens,
a clang of bottles,
the last call at nobody's tavern—
inhaled a last time
exhaled beneath an
unrequited blood moon.

Club Insomnia

A web of fire attaches itself to my predicable
nocturnal rattle of sheets,
as streetlights dim upon darting figments
of sleep disguised as stillness.
Doors open and close, joining me in our nightly ritual—
the party begins,
laughs are hearty and jovial
glasses filled, conversation extraordinary, witty repartee
detours as nighthawks gather.
I turn away from the light
delusions stagger me again and again,
digital glow reminds me of time departed
lost to hours weaving around
the deceased
the forgotten people languish of faith
and the eternal question.

The forecast is vague as daybreak hastens,
was there a moment of slumber or repose?
My companions vanished
diffused by amber sunrise and a tired nod.

I Dream

I dream
in the soft light of darkness
devoid of a chance encounter
in a desert where skies and time slow.

I dream
with one eye open at all times,
as I mold my image into myth
a child lost in an old body—
bells chiming from the clock tower.

When I'm tired
and isolate myself with fury
into a solitary room
amid the help of elders
I decide my fate.
Despite insomnia,
I dream.

CHAPTER 2

California Mythic

Once upon a time a myth unfurled,
under orange surf and ocean drives along
the open and free coastline with few homes
uncluttered mountains
chaparrals and ravines
of diverse wildlife.

But now the days are overcrowded
with angry switchback
freeway slums under homeless skies.
A greedy treaty
as canyon fires scorch ashes in Malibu.
The spotlight is cross-eyed and bewildered.
The beach now overrun with fast paced builders
richly famous and stale from smoggy thirst,
trying to find an escape route before Redwood curtains
of noir angels fall asleep as dreams became
illusions of mud slides and dried aquifers.

The myth became a costly charade
stranded in traffic,
stuck on the fault line—
a golden dystopia
frozen in prehistoric tar pits
as evolution awaits.

Venice

Campo San Polo echoes a child's laughter
off patched bricks
as vivid red and blue laundry
dries between homes along narrow streets.

Parchment geographers meander
as the Grand Canal
disperse time while I say goodbye
to the pigeons of piazza San Marco,
singing fractured opera,
as poets sip espresso in a café—
warmed by the sun
that grows purple bougainvillea
draping from balconies.

Too Much Paris

Rue St. Michel's bridge
above Seine,
rapid current below—
graffiti over Mona Lisa.
Monet underground
rides the Metro.

Montparnasse cigarette café
a smoky haze—
artists wander to look for cheap wine.
I spot Picasso who argues with a prostitute
who slept with Hemingway in the back of
Shakespeare and Company.

Burned books
de Gaulle marching upright
pisses on Nazi goosesteps
down the Champs-Élysées,
G.I. liberates and waves to crowds
later will high kick at the Moulin Rouge.

In Montmartre
Renoir sips champagne with Satie.
Van Gogh frantic with colors is all ears listens to
Toulouse-Lautrec's short argument with Napoleon.

Seine slows
along shadows of the Tuileries—
medieval streets curve
toward jazz guitar and anisette

echo of the lost generation
a movable Arc de Triomphe
while beat generation
lust poetry drunk on music
in the La Marais cafés.

Venus de Milo rides a bicycle
with French bread
under her arms.
King Louie seductive guillotine
captures brief bloody rapture.

Streetwalkers take communion in Notre Dame
from father de Maupassant
who lures them inside the confessional.

Alone in a dim café
Rimbaud
courts a gargoyle
later discovers the sewers
of Andre Breton.

Space aliens receive mystifying signals
from the Eiffel Tower—
capture Salvador Dalí,
who is quickly released
too much
too crazy,

too much Paris.

Mesa Verde

A stumble toward a coral breeze
of cliff dwellers ruins
retrieved on sacred plateaus,
forgotten after draught and diseases.
A white shadow casts on fallen lives,
cling to fragile medicine
tossed on tainted blankets.

Pinyon pine cut and buried
into a maize vision
flatbread fire holy rattle,
slumberous as twilight fades
into a quest of cacti and dreams.
All is sacred.
All is sky and wind
in the dwellers now vanished.

Christmas on the Border

Barbed-wire wreaths twist into
red rock desert canyon.
Pre-fab pink tacos
poked at by sharp forks
turn to dust on plastic plates.
Fluorescent coffee on Spanish napkins
stained by mesquite thorns as
border patrol pistols fire into soft mangers
which ascend into heaven and
burns in a phantom bajada
extinguished by pages
of Ogallala coyote music.

dreams beyond the 100th meridian

radiant silence of clear light
a mosaic of slow circle stars that iridescent winds
push with sagebrush teeth
only a Pawnee ghost dance takes flight
into crystal wilderness
anasazi railroad tracks point toward an empty arroyo
in barren canyons
on singed adobe foothills of the colorado plateau

volcanic turkey vultures
discover a fossil swamp of cold granite roots
red dust red dust red dust red sierra
arid rocks breathe bright pinyon pine
wrapped the barbwire turquoise pueblo
cholla cactus dry riverbed red
emeralds hang from
ancient
redwoods
the spruce cones
sear radiant silence of clear light

Jerusalem Heat

Walled city
of tight streets
Arab shops of pastel clothes
chess sets
and jewelry.

Humorless
heads covered—
tourist scatter
into cafés rising upon Roman streets
Persian sandals and
Egyptian stones,
exodus to Western Wall
separated from ancient children
and nations.

A golden mosque
closed midday
suspicious and guarded.

Lines extend into Church of the Holy Sepulchre
where Constantine wrote fantasies
for the masses—
Via Delarosa never saw a bleeding man,
the Emperor's sleight of hand
a snicker through the ages
the joke is on all of us,
defending what never was—

hot sun blinds sheltered eyes
on the masks of Abraham
lacking water and food
twisted visions
hallucinate
the kind and pious.

The desert needs restoration
from the dogmatic oasis
replant and
replace
open the path
remove the wall.

Yes the sun is delirious.

St. John's Newfoundland

Wood frame homes of plum and mustard
beyond Duckworth Street—
fire survivors of past century.
Scaffold canopy braced on wooden stairs,
plaster and nails restore
houses of 19th-century sea captains
and Water Street shopkeeper streets
lit by gaslight
as streetcars lurch forward.

Hills sink into slim sidewalks of
George Street
whose musicians persuade
the British Islands into North America.
Large iron freighters slowly dock in the harbor.
Men unload cheaply made curios
then descend the metal steps
in search of whiskey.

Water Street once a haven
for whoring and saloons,
criminals and exiled,
cod and whiskey runners
all in search of another dark port,
now sanitized and tidy for the tourist trade.

Unexpected Choices

He drives recklessly into the
Santa Fe wilderness,
barreling over 2 lane roads
swerving past blurred pines
crossing the yellow line
again and again
talking of God.
He locates
the vast crimson illusion
a total
planet
train wreck.

He watches vermilion clouds
rain
fiery switchblades
which burrow underground
mixed with
magenta lichens.

He continues to drive recklessly into
Santa Fe wilderness
gripping the steering wheel
again and again,

swerving past God.

Colorado, 19th Century

I was trying to plow granite soil
with iron blades;
thin atmosphere exhausts me
as I wrestle the horse to a stalemate.
A hard wind throws sand
and sunlight into my eyes
blinded by fatigue.

Why am I here?
No wife or
children to help.
The distant mountains disperse rain clouds
grasses form short interruptions
in taupe starkness.
A train is beyond sight
beyond home.

I am tired and weak
as I sit in a wooden chair
in a darkened room lit with kerosene lanterns
as days pass
feel indistinguishable
counting lifetimes into one.

How far do I go
until today is finished?

Summer Forest

The forest sank like a trance
as fireflies scatter as tadpoles
into the night skies.

I feared the shadow footprint
of a lone wolf,
following my steps
the scent of a ripe kill
as the forest becomes darker
the stars tilt
as the crickets became silent
until the next electric evening.

Sea Turtle

The sea turtle is pondering
near tangled kelp
as he crawls his slow
breath
under water
his fin kicking away the salt—
a scaled eye closes
on sea lava.
He speaks a language
of another eon
under waves
when civilization was
coral reefs and clouds.

Now he gazes
the fleshy legs and arms
taking pictures daily—
knowing his long life
may be shortened due to
the frequent intruders
as civilization encases
its carapace
over the islands.

A Quiet Stroll Through the Roman Forum

Past cultures crumble and bow to our alien feet!

Sacked temples
built by slaves
later fed to lions,
Coliseum shrieks thumbs down
toward a gladiators' shield,
eyes bloody
upon 50,000 barbarians.

Toppled statues and terracotta urns
embrace the House of Vestals.
The conqueror
a mossy earth
swept from pagan heroes and
the winds of Caesar,
beyond their departed gods.

Warren Woods Winter

The continuum of time
since Potawatomi tribes arrived at
a motionless silver-grey forest.
Paths blur beneath a carpet of dried leaves,
a mosaic of moss and pale lichens
hollowed into a frozen waterfall
cut by railroad tracks and farms
on verdant hills.

Muscled ancient beech
extend into waking clouds
and sandy roots,
tap a primeval radiance
that lies on fallen logs
another cycle at the verge of time.

CHAPTER 3

What Would Jim Harrison Say?

He probably wouldn't give a shit
if I didn't hike far in Sleeping Bear Dunes,
nor would he like my poetry much
nice try, kid, he'd laugh.
He'd wonder why I don't drink anymore
no gin or whiskey just green tea.
Pondering my route in the Upper Peninsula
he'd shake his head and smile his gaped-toothed smile
and his stray eye not focusing on anything.
Every footstep I've taken in the woods of Michigan
or deserts in Arizona
wouldn't impress him,
just a car hiker
doesn't hunt or fish
or camp in worn sleeping bags,
hiding my eyes from the moon and stars.

The wolf is here in the understory
of the Porcupine Mountains forest
beneath the bunchberry and bracken ferns,
a good place to die today or any day.
The road home, I asked,
and he points and swings his arms in all directions
you choose, kid, he says,
it's the shape of the journey where a man gives up his name.

Blind Walls of Twisted Love

I met Dante and Beatrice for an expresso
at Café Paradiso.
My unrequited yearning was immense
as we talked past midnight
while the waning moon overhead softened our prudence
and tempered my hopelessness of the erratic spheres.

Faith and fortitude shook my ascent
as a mandolin strummed in the piazza echoing off
blind walls of twisted love.
The wheel turns at a single speed
justified by charity and clarity of the stars.
The soul.
Wise force.
The sheer comedy of the night that merges into
Empyrean light.

Motives

While wandering the sewers of Paris under Rue Montmartre,
pondering a surreal painting by de Chirico, while sipping
anisette—
I spotted Edith Piaf singing *La Vie en Rose*
which echoed into the night tunnels.
She was attempting to find an exit for some fresh air
waving me to join her,
we climbed onto the street and found a café.
She demanded another anisette
while speaking of Yves Montand and his exile from Tuscany.
Patrons recognized her and wondered
why the little sparrow was with me,
perhaps a tryst or just another ragged poet
trying to convince the world of his prophesy.

Edith ignored the people and looked deeply in my eyes
considering my motives,
as I considered hers in boneless light.

Mingus Fight Song
(or The Epitaph of a Jive Ass Saint)

Fury of sounds
a chorus of elegant tone and sudden jolt—
the clown is laughing
and angry
and hurt
in his soul,
fights with phantom spirits.
Laced melody between tender percussion,
a deep bass punctures the tenor saxophones and ride cymbal,
on piano and throaty trombone
for children to hear
total freedom,
a blur of corner angles into one sound
non troppo,
a rapid burst fills the void.

A call and response
in three colors
an orange fable resonance in
trumpet blues
or a cello gentle as a bird settling upon a fisherman's string
pulled closer to death
through a chill of a hurricane.

Don’t be afraid,
we’re all afraid too
including the clown.

Sun Ra

I asked Sun Ra,
is space really the place?
He turned his head from the keyboard
his sequined cape and skull cap
sparkled into cosmic fury,
“Crazy man, the place is space
nothing but black infinity.”
He was hitting notes
past the range of human sound.

His accompanying dancers were
melting intergalactic ice caps
station to station.
Vibrating sounds of spheres
on the other side of music.

I sipped my scotch
as he played,
he glanced at me once or twice
as the nightclub
began a turbulent shaking
without percussion and beyond truth.

I looked out the window,
lights were flashing
and Rush Street began to fade
becoming more distant
as we bolted away
from the foundations of the club
into orbit where
the place is really space,
the variable universe.
Crazy man.

What Do You Think?

What do you think Ernest?
men marry men
women marry women.

It's a new day Ernest,
steady yourself
with a strawberry daiquiri.

Did you ever consider you and F. Scott
alone
kissing
that would drive Zelda jealous
where she wouldn't complain
about her husband's sexual prowess.

Give it a try Ernest,
what the hell you live in Key West
there's plenty of action on the pier.
Your friend Gertrude seems happy.

You seem to be pissed Ernest,
ready to get your shotgun
or give me a left hook,
maybe I better leave.

Come on Ernest,
what do you really think?

Open Mic

I've seen the best minds of my generation
destroyed by poetry readings
—Lawrence Ferlinghetti

The poet took a short step upon
the narrow platform
no microphone is needed in the tight café
as he begins to read
not sure if he wants to do stand-up,
poetry,
or a therapy session.
He attempts an unsuccessful blend of all.

I sip my coffee wishing for some bourbon.
Looking at my watch
and the shabby audience
like riders on the El at 2am
rambling through the night.
I'm hoping for a quick ending
but another page is recited.

There's an increase of rustling
as his final stanza or one liner
settles on the now sparse crowd,
a truly relieved and perfunctory applause.
Now my name is called to read,
I take one last sip of coffee
and head out the door.

Heart Attack

Sitting and waiting in the ER,
the pain in his chest fluctuates on an invisible scale,
sharp and dull.
“In a moment” the nurse says.
He nods and understands what is happening to him.
“Give me a cigarette. This might be my last one for a while,” he says to his wife.
She hands him one and he lights up,
a shallow drag, a muffled cough.
She joins him with a smoke.
“The doctor’s ready to see you,” the nurse returns.
As he walks into the examination room
all ashtrays are filled.

The nights seem trapped in an EKG screen.
Jagged lines follow a breath,
a skipped beat,
not yet, not now, he says silently to nobody in the room.

Oasis

An orphan is never alone.
The blind piano tuner is vibrating a quiet breath
that could shape the consciousness of empathy.
A night watchman strolls in shadows to reach between
sharp silhouettes of a spiked palm near a waterfall.

The piano tuner had perfect pitch
in the motel in El Cajon desert
as night skies black with vibrational tone
frame a palm oasis.

The orphan cried into the evening
his ghost mother rocked him and he slept fitfully until twilight,
as the night watchman made his final rounds before dawn and
disappeared in a frenzy of desire.

John Cage Writes a Poem

Wired to cactus spines plunk
melodious into night air.
A siren echoes then fades into
a profusion of silence
4 minutes and 33 seconds—
only ambient breath.
On the street below
the hum of traffic and
occasional shuffling of feet
on the sidewalk.

Zen strumming of notes
minimalist rhythm ringed octave
Tao stars sing a rubric fable—
knit a limpid night sky.
A piano key reverberates into a holy relic
of empty space only to dazzle
a vast whisper on blank pages.

Oliver and Collins

I met Mary and Billy at an upscale coffee house.
They sat together at a nearby table
both smiled at me, but Mary dodged her eyes.
"You both write such clear and uncluttered poems," I said.
"Simple with no pretense or vague meanings,
sometimes a subtle joke."

"Analyze a poem and you lose it," Mary said. And Billy nodded.
Mary sipped her mint tea and Billy had another café latte.
I attempted another question, and both ignored it.
They soon began talking to each other
speaking a language I couldn't comprehend
laughed heartily and then left
without a goodbye or saying a word.

As I finished my coffee,
I pondered their exits.
Simple, uncomplicated and perhaps a subtle joke.

Dex

A return from Parisian coffeehouses
and electric espresso.
His respite from Jim Crow sheet music.

Tonight tables are filled with
polka dots and moonbeams.

Golden tenor saxophone
takes repeated bows
from a standing room
of blue notes.

Crowds line Rush Street
for the second show and the third.
Showcase Siegel eyes the audience,
years of lost dollars returned tonight in his smoky club.

Long tall Dex
in society red relaxes
blowing solos into
the wee small hours of the morning.

Dostoyevsky

I spoke to Dostoyevsky
about the revolution,
he laughed dewy eyed
and banged his fist upon the table.
Bourgeois, goddamn bourgeois,
the man spewed.
Lenin was fool,
Gogol a idiot,
and James Joyce an Irish fraud.

I told him your stories are too long
too depressing
too much sorrow.
Bourgeois, goddamn bourgeois
he bellowed.

Chekhov was a joke,
Hemingway a communist
all the rest phony intellectuals.

He tipped over the table
spills cheap vodka
and stained papers.

There are no answers or easy conclusions
to the Czar and his army.

Bourgeois, I am a goddamn bourgeois.
He sighed.

Therapy for T.S.

Thomas it's time to relax.
Let go of your despair and dispossession
the hollow men can go their own way.
Play another game of chess.
The humid God snaking down the river,
did you forget your roots?

Timeless time is one.
Let us go you and I to seek some peace
as music surrenders in rhythms and lyrics—
tie sorrow to fire and knot.
Silence the mocking voices
a negation of now,
allow depression to sink in the church of Cambridgeshire,
obliquely walk away into
the clouds of unknowing.

CHAPTER 4

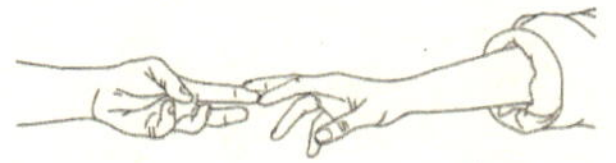

Strangers Again

Incredible lovers suddenly depart
to become strangers again—
highway of the future becomes
the wind chimes of nostalgia.
A terror of silent rain in Big Sur is deafening
above a quiet breath in a snug violet dusk.

An overhead fan rotates in the full moon sky,
under the irony of stars.
Lucid dreams float beyond a rattled night.
I favor an allure in pure solitude
with an eye cocked toward pleasures
in early morning mist of an epic dread
when we become strangers again.

Evolution

When did petroglyphs become algorithms?
Another evolution of language from hunters
to modern gatherers.
The propagation memory of tribal ghosts.

Petroglyphs on the subway walls—
algorithms for melting ice caps.
Who deciphers the hieroglyphics of ancient souls who knew
time—
yet ultimately misplaced it.

Petroglyphs are meaningless to riders who
only know their stops on trains
leave and return
in a snarl of rank darkness
quick and easy.

A healing waits in the shadows for another sign.

Endless Time Vacant Time

Coral reef salty
tongue of turtle sky
fishing in a paper sea
as snow melts
white into brown
onto graves
of forgotten relatives
waiting to speak
torn and folded upon
grey sunsets.

Today is yesterday, tomorrow is now, the past yet to come
endless time vacant time
time to render myself with
straw mind
a stuttering blank face through coiled wires
whisper in a child's ear
an internal flood of questions.

Desire of a fantasy
sway beyond
satin chain link fence
sealed shut
as wretched wheels skid.

Slowed by
dry rains and
shallow fears
in burnt fields of prairie sage
under orange vapor of soft planets.

Midnight Sunburst

Midnight sunburst
a butcher blue urgency
perfect for an insomniac pontificator
rattling profane bliss.

Marble masks meander
under a snug violet twilight
as incidental music slides
an eternal maze of mayhem
into liquid slumber.

The ring of earthly bells
a skyless fluorescence of lucid blush
a dawn song of celestial intemperance.

Planet

Earth's craters
behind blinders of Anthropocene era—
a lifeless twilight of inferno breezes
as glaciers backslide
on parched cosmic soil
a tormented meteoroid lingers
upon beaches of plankton seas.

A fossil chain of recycled hydrogen
facing an icy dilemma into
dim distant sun
of ammonia sky and cathartic ocean.

A solitary buzzard with frozen wings
circles the equator following winds
blinded by evolutionary frost that
awaits human language
after the sixth extinction.

Chaos Theory

The butterflies are back!
After a milkweed resonates
thunder and catastrophe,
butterflies are revived.

Confined as we are,
disoriented in space
shifts in the tides,
wax and wane of the moon,
butterfly wings jolt the earth and its timeline,
confront chaos theory in the eyes of giants
who turn the wheels
that turn the screws
away from
our lingering existence.

Visitation

Time becomes a pixilated memory
of bliss and blood
as the clock winds down.

We pause to visit for a brief daze
as the foundation weakens
while wonders compress
into petrified shadows
a maze of a riveting plot
elapsed in repetition
as the evening strides
and blur into all other days.

A Late Fate

Seas fossilize into parched buttes
trapped shellfish
arthropods in dark matter.

Time did not freeze
as a massive ice ball
and volcanoes
merge into passive resistance
push and pull
on earth axis.

The bacteria count is one.

A shock of celestial proportions,
life is a stunning pool of
bombarded asteroid ice
melting eons
upon eons
until the surf is up
the sun is down
and sulfur tide pools
froze hominids in their tracks.

Enough is enough
when will the party begin?

River Run

Riverrun past James
believe me it does
boats beyond timepiece curtains
there is no wake on the river.
Riverrun
terrified run
until the endless dry headstones
dam the cloudyphiz river.

an enigmatic trap door
opens
to a timeless dream death
Riverrun at times
without an intricate Druidia
twist into fragments
of enlightened him
saintly laughter and punman
a shuttered riddle
sinagains fake
for the final
Riverrun.

Reckoning

The last regions of the world
dissolved into a feudal spiral
and quiet death march
before the lie caught up with the mighty oath.

Walking toward the intrepid mirrors,
a masking of ideas
that mimic a genius woven into a masquerade.
I wonder if it's all on the level
or to confuse us as the curtain comes down
to sting and slice before the final scene.

Staggering into a wracked excuse
as the somber night slams into daybreak.
My pulse accelerates into a shaman quest of time
as the desert bleeds
held together by a mirage
betrayed beyond reflection
repeats a sleight of hand rebellion.

Yes the moment has come.

Glass Vertigo

Under glass
under siege
as others warp and twist their necks
amazed at my tightrope dance—
a sideshow of spinning plates.

Only I see the mirrored hallways,
the trap doors, angular balance
mystery calcium carbonate crystals
cling to an air tight channel,
a millimeter in scope
the gelatin membrane holds
vestibule blood
fumbling an attempt to balance
what was formerly steady
for a new life challenge—
on tilted sidewalks
longing for a shattering of
invisible glass
below vertigo skies.

Conception

Mutations and division of seeds
unite with a cast of
spiritcells
karmic genes
create all of us
since evolution's slow crawl
from the swamps.

Secrets whispered into my inner ear
on a late October evening,
an instant leap of trust
where a mysterious life force
settled upon the streets of Chicago
where mutations and division of seeds
unite with a cast of
spiritcells
and karmic genes
creating all
embrace in a tumbled plunge
into a miraculous glow.

Diagnosis

Russian roulette with a
rusty pistol
walking blind
on a frayed rope
above toxic waters
slow and unseen.

The loss is immense
without a glance,
all sunrises departed
but longed for.

A murmur
that irritated before
now a kiss of forgiveness,
atonement
a silent plea
gives hope
or death—
the air thick with soot
a sidewalk slippery and
perilous
yet I still meander
with one eye closed
yearning for a remission
of fear.

Last Rites

I took time off from work.

The grave was dug by strangers
who buried a loved one
below life's cold memory.
All have grown away
a wheezing end
of another early morning demise.

Time meanders in capricious confusion
huddled by an erratic guillotine
which has the final laugh
into the vaporous night,
as fragrant jasmine alert the gathering
to the great and glorious
clouds of refuge.

CHAPTER 5

The El

Vertical steel lace
curving over streets
and alleys
a horizontal
Eiffel Tower
on elevated veins
of late 19th century
cross-braced
above shadows and
angular bits of sunlight.

Rivets
intersect and thread
slow-motion rails
around wooden platforms
as metal tokens
and windblown transfers
among phantom riders of murky intrigue
who land onto their stops.

Dappled city of light
points backward
rattles forward
along rust-washed
Lake Street
ghost factories.

The third rail thunders
past labyrinths of

grey wooden stairs and porches
with faded advertisements painted
on brick walls
of apartments.

Staccato rhythm
every five minutes
El tower miles long
props itself up
from moist prairie asphalt.

Water Crib 1948

Three miles from shore
only splashing waves,
hum of motors and chained wheels—
accidental music in sunrise fog.

He begins the day at a brink of time
with coffee and writes into a notebook
a solitary Dharma bum in Lake Michigan
a week at a time.
The sunlight reflects jewels upon the water,
silence deaf as a yawn
as pages mattered more than the turning of cranks
and repeated dial readings with
walkie-talkie static in a rusty toolbox.
His notebook is filled with boxers and speed bags
taped knuckles and broken-down fears
in desolate neighborhoods.

A motorboat approaches from shore upon a dusky wind
ready to change workers for the week.
Stepping on a broken ladder onto the boat
he left his retreat until next week as
the wind and choppy waves stagger him
a seasick blood
taking his licks but not ready to forfeit.

Nightman at the Conservatory

All crowds and workers have left the Victorian crystal garden.

Flashlight shines on deep fragrance of Hyacinth spring
and moist soil as I make my rounds
in February behind the darkened greenhouse door.
Steam pipes rattle and pound—
water falls in the pond from a concrete urn
surrounded by lush philodendron foliage.

Rooms change temperatures suddenly
as cold slams into humidity.
A large iron circular wheel is cranked sending
a rush of stream into the main pipe
warms the Palm House dome.
Steel pillars flower,
pipes hammer
sharp and loud,
damp rust elongates
vanilla vines and palm roots.

Muted streetlights of Stockton Drive extend inside the
Conservatory
as snow mats dried lawns and conceal bare branches in the park.

Sometimes extra plants casually slip out
the back metal door,
undetected in dim shadows.

The potting range is lit from humming fluorescent bulbs
hanging by chain over concrete benches
where dry soil is neatly piled
clay pots stacked to one side.

The light fades as greenhouse after greenhouse is checked—
55 degrees
68 degrees
45 degrees
one pipe turned off under a side bench
another overhead pipe turned on filling with steam
reverberates and taps rhythmically
metal on metal.

An open greenhouse door slams unexpectantly.

Reflections on glass
two flashlights appear
Am I alone?

Yes,
all have left hours ago.

All will return in the morning.

Beach 1958

A short
trolley bus ride along
Montrose Avenue
to Broadway,
end of the line.

A long
three block walk
to the beach
past brick apartments,
pulling my mother's hand
until the trees and park
are visible.

The sand is hot
the lake is cold

but it doesn't matter.

Near the beach
a white Nike Missile station looms
behind a cyclone fence
radiates
a constant hum
of the radar antennae
which rotates slowly,

but it doesn’t matter,

splashing is fun
waving to mom.

A long shadow
casts upon America 1958
people gaze at the
black and white sky
with plastic sunglasses
in wonder
and fear,

but it doesn’t matter,

tuna sandwich tastes good,
sun is warm in living color.

Lake Michigan

Sluggish prairie floodplain
a Pottawattamie
canoe vanishes into
white musket powder
strange hair and teeth
of Fort Dearborn.

she-ca-gu
the stinking onion,
deceptive soft blue summer
a graveyard under Lake Mishigami gales
of wooden schooners and steamship wrecks
a final resting spot for tanks and bodies
intermingle among 1871 fire ravaged rubbish.

Multitude of hands
cut ditches
reverse heavy
sewer syrup
away from the sipping blue lake
and Chicago River of cholera
later flushed down stream.

Cut timber from Wisconsin forests
unknown bundles tangled and dropped
conceal evidence

secretly at midnight
sink fleetingly to sandy lake bottom
scattering sturgeon large and meaty
trout and perch.

Bottles, cans and iron safes
raw sludge from steel mills and factories—
a lone drunken cry for help on a party yacht
dark sunglasses float away
too late for help.

It's been 14,000 years
since skies warmed glaciers to reveal
moist flat sunrise
filling with ground water and rain
dug without shovels
ready to swallow
illusions and souls.

Lincoln Avenue Noir

The Apache Motel curtains closed
as a table lamp glows in the double-locked room,
cars parked clandestinely in the lot
another night of wonder.

Down the block the Guest House hourly patrons
women in short skirts call out to a boy on a bicycle
pedaling hard down Bryn Mawr Avenue
to escape the echoed call.

The O-Mi Motel retreats into bygone days
of Route 66,
neon flashing throughout the night,
maps folded into the glove compartment
once on outskirts of the city—
fresh ice and color TV
in every room.

The Summit Motel swimming pool
is paved over to extend parking,
the tattooed lady is gone
since the green shag carpets
on another affair of freedom.

The Rio Motel has waterbeds not known in the 50s
black lingerie dropped to the floor-
cash transaction

as small packages are swiftly exchanged,
a rod rests on the table
as the pizza boy knocks and delivers a hot one.

At the police station built after
another leaky-faucet motel
is torn down,
cops shrug their shoulders
at the parked cars and dim lights inside rooms
where the couples hurriedly peer over their shoulders
as they head into rooms of cracked tiles
and peeling wallpaper,
before hurriedly inserting a key into the lock.
He tells her—
you can't hit a moving target.

Graceland Cemetery

Springtime amongst time
gated in small patches of
black granite
eternal silence
span three centuries,
as lichens crawl
over headstones.
Ancient gallery of the city dead
recognizable names of streets,
schools and unknown histories.
Abolitionists and underground railroad conductors
dodging diseases and gunshots
escape from fires and floods,
con men in disguise.

A sudden retreat from a swampy lakefront burial ground
into green plots surrounded by horse drawn carts
on dirt roads.

Daniel Burnham eyes the lagoon
on an island of ashes
who converted wetlands
into a Ferris wheel in a white city of wonder.

Louis Sullivan sharpened pencil and muddy boots fade
unto restless prairie arches build
upon drunken T-square evenings.

Mies van der Rohr stark gravestone
rests near a neatly cut lawn
displaced Jim Crow refugees
from ghetto apartments.

Roman columns protect a tyrant
from Pullman railroad calloused men
with angry fists,
who cannot afford to die here.

As the El rattles
alongside graves and mausoleums
every 10 minutes.

Philip Armour workers' sharp
cleavers carve
socialist union dreams
while Haymarket rioters freeze
before billy-clubs and bombs
tear into the crowd
spared by Governor Altgeld.

Stone pyramid
mausoleum of a beer brewer
poured into working class saloons as
politicians cluster together in cigar
smoke as Jack Johnson
toss punches on a bloody white hope.

Crowds cheer in the sun of
segregated bloodlines
as Hulbert's National League
dead ball cheers
among former slaves in unmarked graves
as summer street cars snarl
with bootleggers and fancy girls.

The placid lagoon dredged from an ancient beach
welcome visitors of three centuries,
alive and dead on arrival.

As the El rattles
alongside graves and mausoleums
every 10 minutes.

Empty Greenhouse

Empty
in an empty greenhouse.
After a season of growth ready for public view
Cyclamen
Cineraria and the
scent of *Jasmine,*
now algae-stained circles remain
from salty terra cotta pots
once lined in rows
on the flat concrete bench.

I watch sunlight through falling snow
separated by glass,
in silent afternoon light—
now under crusty frost.

A hose drips
while a spray of mist
settled like crystal beads
on lank transparent leaves.

Peeling white paint on vertical metal steam pipeline
a hollow rattle as circular valves open
below the benches as
steam pipes breathe warmth
sending a rush of heat as dry vapor
settles on side windows.

A dented water can
with a bent nozzle—

rubber apron and black boots
hang by a locker—
dry curled leaves
once scattered on a bench,
cut banana leaves
in a dumpster
return to compost,
as a door closes while
I prepare for the next crop
in an empty greenhouse.

On Vacation

To Florida for two weeks,
leaving two turtles
in a filled bathtub—
a large white reflected pool
as tiny green carapaces swim,
a temporary jail break
away from the small circular bowl
so little water
so little space.

In the light of
morning frosted glass
and summer warmth
the lost DNA of swamps and rocks
returns
with freedom
exhilarating freedom,
in this new habitat
where the only predator
is the drain.

Chicago Farrago

City of the century
which century?
City on the make
sleight of hand mysterious
Chi-town, not a windy city.
Century of progress spans a Third Coast
World's fair of illusions and death traps
doorways in a White City.

Blue note on fire and flung into the lake,
Empire room rumbles under the El
City of Broad Shoulders,
a fortified machine of parades and green river of sloth.
Sewers of entrails floating belly up to the sunbaked skies,
Palmer House near Lord Montgomery's lakefront
cobblestone rails flatten into tunnels
of a labyrinth speakeasy,
drinks are on me in this toddling town of
a bewildered Carrie typing alone into the night.
The push and pull of black and white shadows
in bungalows of a lost city.

Bughouse is not for squares,
the Old Town is watching
behind blinders to stop the presses and factories.
My kind of town, but who are you?

I know a guy who knows a guy
but don't send nobody nobody sent
to Graceland graveyard
up on Rosehill by the lagoons of Oakwoods.

A skyscraper of cemeteries packed with victims and predators
saintly ward healers laugh your troubles away
in a city that works for time-clock artists and burglars in blue.
Downbeat downtown under siege,
riots undulating in time warp of hope
transplanted by Jim Crow soul trains crisscross
late night London House jazz piano.

Chicago windows peer out to prairie riverview reversing
anarchists near neon water towers
and steel mills of green lunch buckets.
Paved gravel Haymarket roads span poverty
a glimpse of the lake from tip top tap
upon a flyover of literary renaissance on
world's busiest street corner underground,
conventions bleakly stop during the Silent City
a sweet home as coyotes prowl unattended Second City as
another film loop rolls,
Potawatomi city in a garden
as Mother Cabrini blesses all
unmarked headstones
in the sleepless city.

NOTES

Invasive Accident

Tree frogs, *Pseudacris regilla,* native to western Canada and United States.

Blind Walls of Twisted Love

Influenced by Dante's allegory poem, *The Divine Comedy,* specifically *Paradiso,* the third and final section of his epic work.

John Cage Writes a Poem

4 minutes 33 seconds is a composition by John Cage (1912–1992) in which performers are instructed to remain silent. Its meaning demonstrates there is no true silence. The ambient sounds of the environment become the music. It premiered in 1952 and was met with shock and widespread controversy.

Dex

Joe Siegel (1926–2020) was the owner of the Jazz Showcase, one of Chicago's oldest jazz clubs open since 1947. It has been in several different locations.

Chaos Theory

In chaos theory, a minute localized change (a butterfly flapping its wings) can have a large effect in a complex system, triggering a series of events that can lead to a significant outcome.

River Run

Wordplay motivated from *Finnegan's Wake* by James Joyce.

Chicago Farrarago

Inspired by Nelson Algren's prose poem "City on the Make."

About the Author

John Raffetto's poetry is published in print and online and has been nominated for a Pushcart Prize. John holds degrees from the University of Illinois and Northeastern Illinois University. He worked as a horticulturalist and landscape designer for many years at the Chicago Park District. Its conservatories and parks were an inspirational environment for poems concerning nature, people, and the city. He's also worked as an adjunct professor, and taught classes at museums, libraries, and botanic gardens. A lifelong resident of Chicago, he lives with his wife, and they have an adult son.

www.ingramcontent.com/pod-product-compliance
Lightning Source LLC
LaVergne TN
LVHW090616110826
845146LV00001B/407

* 9 7 9 8 9 0 1 4 6 8 2 0 3 *